KT-177-344

LOST *in* TRANSLATION

Løst in Tränšlatioπ

Misadventures in English Abroad

CHARLIE CROKER

Illustrations by Louise Morgan

MICHAEL O'MARA BOOKS LIMITED

First published in Great Britain in 2006 by
Michael O'Mara Books Limited
9 Lion Yard, Tremadoc Road
London SW4 7NQ

Copyright © Charlie Croker 2006

Illustrations © Louise Morgan 2006
for www.artmarketillustration.com

The right of Charlie Croker to be identified as the author of this
work has been asserted by him in accordance with the Copyright,
Designs and Patents Act 1988.

All rights reserved. No part of this publication may be reproduced,
stored in a retrieval system, or transmitted by any means, without
the prior permission in writing of the publisher, nor be otherwise
circulated in any form of binding or cover other than that in which
it is published and without a similar condition including this
condition being imposed on the subsequent purchaser.

A CIP catalogue record for this book
is available from the British Library

ISBN (10-digit): 1-84317-208-9
ISBN (13-digit): 978-1-84317-208-6

5 7 9 10 8 6 4

www.mombooks.com

Designed and typeset by Martin Bristow

Printed and bound in Great Britain by Clays Ltd, St Ives plc

Contents

———

Acknowledgements

I am very grateful to the Hoffnung Partnership for permission to quote several replies from German hotels, which the late Gerard Hoffnung immortalized in his 1958 speech to the Oxford Union. (This is available as a BBC recording, *Hoffnung: A Last Encore.*)

Many thanks to Louise Morgan for her illustrations. In some cases I think they should replace the original signs.

Thanks are also due to the following for their intrepid efforts in the name of research: Kerry Duckworth, Nigel Farndale, Norman Geras, Markus Grupp, Marie Gumaelius, Rob Heeley, Chris Hope, Alison Lindsay, John Melbourne, Chris Pavlo and Mark Schuck.

It's customary for authors to conclude their acknowledgements with the disclaimer that any errors which follow are entirely their fault. Please understand why I'm not doing that here.

CHARLIE CROKER
July 2006

Introduction

━━━

YOU'RE in a far-flung corner of the globe, it's the early hours of the morning and you've just checked into your hotel after an exhausting flight. The prospect of a seven-thirty business breakfast is filling you with dread, and you've a nagging feeling you forgot to pack your toothbrush. Very little seems right with the world. But then you notice a sign in the corner of the bathroom: 'Please to bathe inside the tub.' Despite your tiredness, you can't help but smile. Yes – you're *Lost in Translation.*

All over the world, from Beijing to Buenos Aires, in hotels and restaurants and taxis and zoos (yes, zoos), these priceless nuggets of verbal dottiness lie in wait, ready to brighten the lives of the jaded voyagers who chance upon them. They are the reward points on our Travel loyalty card. They are the treats we earn for enduring mislaid luggage, deep-vein thrombosis and stony-faced stewardesses. Never failing to amuse, they put a spring in our step with nothing more complicated than an off-balance vocabulary and some iffy syntax. It's English, Jim, but not as we know it.

Sometimes you can tell what was meant: 'Our wine list leaves you nothing to hope for.' Sometimes you can't: 'Nobody is allowed to sit on the both sides of the boat.'

Sometimes you're not sure whether you can tell or not: the Indian hotel, for instance, that warns 'No spiting on the walls.' Is that 'spitting' or 'writing'? If the former, why only on the walls? A hotel in Beijing tells guests they have 'No permission to wench.' Is this a deliberately invented verb, a discreet euphemism for the professional activities of a certain kind of lady? Or do they mean something else? If so, what? 'Wrench'? But what could you wrench in a hotel room? The mind boggles.

Other entries belong firmly in the 'How did *that* happen?' file. The fake Liverpool FC shirts in China, for example, which have meticulously copied every last detail, right down to the club crest . . . and then turned 'You'll Never Walk Alone' into 'You'll Never Pickle Again'. Occasionally you're left in doubt as to whether the language is wrong or not. A notice in one Shanghai hotel reads: 'It is forbidden to play the recorder in guest rooms.' Do they really mean 'recorder'? If so, *why?* Has there been an epidemic of people playing that instrument? Do the Chinese take particular offence at it, even more than we do? Is that possible?

The beauty of getting lost in translation is that you never know where you'll end up. Some examples mess with your head: 'If you wish, you may open the window. Do not open the Window.' Some are inadvertently beautiful: 'Little grass is smiling slightly, please walk on the pavement.' Some verge on philosophy: 'Danger comes soonest when it's despised.' But whatever the effect, a chuckle is never far away.

A final word of caution. Amused as we are by other nations' fumblings with our language, we should never forget that their English is infinitely better than our Thai/Polish/Vietnamese. Indeed, sometimes it's better than our English – you'll find several examples in these pages from English-speaking nations, whether from the land of Shakespeare or the Land of the Free.

So enjoy. Go forth, take the plunge . . . and get thoroughly *Lost in Translation.*

Have you spotted something you'd like to see included in the next volume of Lost in Translation*? An item on a menu, an instruction leaflet, a hotel notice? If so, we'd love to hear from you:* lostintranslation@virgin.net

Plane Speaking

You're heading for a world where the English language has been tweaked a little. The first signs come before you've even landed . . .

Air China brochure:

Dear Passenger, Wish you have a joyful journey!
When you are in public talking and laughing and
drinking and singing living a happy life, suddenly you
feel some part of your body is too itchy to endure.
How embarrassed! Please dial fax 01-491-02538,
you will gain an unexpected result.

Chinese in-flight magazine:

We'd like to offer our affection as a gift by the white
bird on sky to every genuinely go the same may
together with you. This is our only requite to you.

And another:

Besides, try to prepare all you need before pack, and then, you can arrange everything's position entirely, or you will make yourself confusion.

Instructions on a Korean flight:

Upon arrival at Kimpo and Kimahie Airport, please wear your clothes.

Aeroflot advert:

Introducing wide boiled aircraft for your comfort.

Caption in a Chinese in-flight magazine, underneath a picture of a kilt-wearing bagpipe player:

A man dressed in a Scottish woolen skirt blowing air whistle.

Job recruitment advert for Nok Air airline, Thailand:

If you are energetic, living, friendly . . .

Danish airline:

We take your bags
and send them in all directions.

*Chapter title from a book about the history
of the Garuda airline, Indonesia:*

Total Quality Qontrol.

On an airsickness bag on a Spanish aeroplane:

Bags to be use in case of sickness
or to gather remains.

Things don't look that much better on the ground . . .

*Notice on a broken turnstile at Salzburg,
Austria, passport control:*

Out of work.

Sign at a Beijing airport café:

Welcome greet Presence.

Restaurant in Ben Gurion Airport, Israel:

Payment Before Ordering.

On a luggage trolley at Singapore airport:

Not to be removed from Crewe Station.

Sign on a metal-detector scanner in France:

People with peace-maker do not pass.

*But let's not forget – you don't have to travel abroad
to get lost in translation . . .*

At Heathrow Airport, London, UK:

No electric people carrying vehicles past this point.

Room for Improvement

You've negotiated the flight, you've battled your way through the airport — now you head for the single most prolific source of dodgy English known to mankind: the hotel. The fun starts before you even get to your room . . .

Qatar:

Please do not use the lift when it is not working.

In a hotel lobby, Beijing, China:

Good apperance please no watermelon please.

Paris, France:

Please leave your values at the front desk.

Pingyao, China:

Gussethouse.

Bishek, Kyrgyzstan:

No entries in upper clothes.

Seoul, South Korea:

Third floor: Turkey Bath.

Zurich, Switzerland:

We have nice bath and are very good in bed.

Name of a hotel in Lectoure, France:

Hotel de Bastard.

Czechoslovakia:

Take one of our horse-driven city tours.
We guarantee no miscarriages.

Thailand (offering donkey rides):

Would you like to ride on your own ass?

Baghdad, Iraq:

No consummation whatever
may take place in this foyer.

Africa:

You may choose between a room
with a view on the sea
or the backside of the country.

Amalfi, Italy:

Suggestive views from every window.

Bucharest, Romania:

The lift is being fixed for the next day.
During that time we regret that you will
be unbearable.

Leh, India:

The Old Ladakh Guest House
(hospitalizing since 1974).

Seoul:

Choose twin bed or marriage size;
we regret no King Kong size.

Japan:

City Hotel & Nut Club.

India:

Welcome to Hotel Cosy:
where no one's stranger.

In a hotel cloakroom, Berlin, Germany:

Please hang yourself here.

Cambodian hotel chain:

Aggressive Hotels.

*In the lobby of a Moscow hotel across from
a Russian Orthodox monastery:*

You are welcome to visit the cemetery
where famous Russian and Soviet composers, artists,
and writers are buried daily except Thursdays.

In a Tokyo hotel laundry room:

To everyone of the use, Laundromat –

Many people use a Laundromat. Let's comply with the next item to use it for the cleanness safety.

1. Let's read the explanation of the way of using it well, and use the washing machine, the dryness machine properly.

2. Let's wash a hand well before and after a wash.

3. Don't wash the person who get's an epidemic, and clothes which contacted with the person.

4. Don't wash a diaper which urine stuck to, sports shoes, an animal's rug because an unpleasantness is given to the person handled later and it is un-sanitation.

5. Let's bring it back after you spread the wash from the dryness machine and a state is done.

6. Please ask a satellite control person in charge for the inquiry about the establishment, the contact of in case of emergency.

Sign in the courtyard of a Barcelona hotel, Spain:

No automobiles, Pederosts only.

Istanbul, Turkey:

Flying water in all rooms.
You may bask in sun on patio.

In an Italian hotel, signs by the bell:

If service is required, give two strokes
to the maid and three to the waiter.

It is kindly requested from our guests
that they avoid dirting and doing rumours
in the rooms.

Hot and cold water running up
and down the stairs.

*Left your values? And indeed your watermelon?
Good. You may now proceed to your room – where
yet more delights await . . .*

Ethiopia:

To call room service, please to open door
and call Room Service. Please call quiet,
people may sleep.

On a hotel television set, Belgrade, Serbia:

If set breaks, inform manager.
Do not interfere with yourself.

Indonesia:

Someday laundry service.

Torremolinos, Spain:

Take Discotheque with or without date,
in summer plus open air bonging bar.

Cairo, Egypt:

On September 30, winter timing will start.
As of 12:00 midnight all clocks will be forward
one hour back.

Tokyo, Japan:

Is forbitten to steal hotel towels please.
If you are not person to do such thing
is please not to read notis.

Shanghai, China:

It is forbidden to play the recorder in guest rooms.

Las Palmas, Canary Islands:

If you telephone for room service you will get the answer you deserve.

Milan, Italy:

Our barmen will be pleased to suggest you the menu selection in the intimate atmosphere of the bar Caffe Doria or in the quiteness of your room.

Notice by a phone, Amsterdam, the Netherlands:

Telephone instructions can be found on the backside.

Italy:

Unfortunately the Hotel is not endowed with restaurant.

In a Tokyo hotel bathroom:

Volume on. Squelch. Please dial to shut whenever you want to.

Rome, Italy:

Please dial 7 to retrieve your auto from the garbage.

Budapest, Hungary:

All rooms not denounced by twelve o'clock will be paid for twicely.

Hamburg, Germany:

It is our intention to pleasure you every day.

Tokyo:

Guests are requested not to smoke or do other disgusting behaviours in bed.

T'aipei, Taiwan:

If there is anything we can do to assist
and help you, please do not contact us.

Vietnam:

Visitor should be not carried: arm,
pets of material should be fired into the hotel.
Visitor should be not ironed-cooked-washed.
Hotel has got every service for a visitor.

Guangdong, China:

We serve you with hostiality.

Seoul:

Measles not included in room charge.

Weifang, China:

Invisible service is available for your rest
being not disturbed.

Seeduwa, Sri Lanka:

Harold Tribune is available at lobby paper rack.

Brunei:

Please keep shutters close or monkey make you crazy.

Seoul:

If you wish, you may open the window.
Do not open the Window.

Sri Racha, Thailand:

No in the room.

Dalat, Vietnam:

LAUNDRY BAG

19: Skirt

20: Stocking

21: Hand Kerchief

22: Big Towel

23: Small Towel

24: Hat

25: Shoes

26: Tie

27: Price of ironing

28: Car with 12 to 14 seats

29: Car with 4 seats.

Thailand:

At the cashier's counter kindly note
that personal cheese are not accepted.

Serbia:

Voltage is 220 V but the use of the electric i rous
or telt les is not permitted.

Also in Serbia:

For schedube and programmes of theaters
as well as the tickets for all the types of performances,
please, consult (he hall parter).

Bangkok, Thailand:

Please maintain temperature at 1 degree from 25,
any higher or lower will only make the room
hotter or colder.

Italy:

This hotel is renowned for its peace and solitude.
In fact, crowds from all over the world
flock here to enjoy its solitude.

Bosnia:

Guests should announce the abandonment of their
rooms before 12 o'clock, emptying the room at
the latest until 14 o'clock, for the use of the room
before 5 at the arrival or after the 16 o'clock at
the departure, will be billed as one night more.

*In a bed-and-breakfast establishment
near Giverny, France:*

Welcome in your home.

We are pleased to share with you our way of living.
Please listen to these few words.

The genuine antics in your room come from
our family castle. Long life to it.

Please avoid coca watering, cream cleaning,
wet towels wrapping and ironing drying.
For your linen we have at your disposal garden
and ironing facilities.

Due to our location in the countryside, care not
to throw anything (no rubber) in the toilet (WC).

Don't hesitate to use the terrace or the lounge.
More comfortable than a bar in your bed.

Have a nice stay. We'll do our best to please you and
help you discovering French typical surroundings.

Sorrento, Italy:

The concierge immediately for informations.
Please don't wait last minutes.
Then it will be too late to arrange
any inconveniences.

Leipzig, Germany:

Ladies, please rinse out your teapots standing
upside down in sink. In no event should
hot bottoms be placed on counter.

Ankara, Turkey:

Please hang your order before retiring
on your doorknob.

India:

No spiting on the walls.

Tel Aviv, Israel:

If you wish breakfast, lift the telephone
and our waitress will arrive. This will be enough
to bring up your food.

Madrid, Spain:

If you wish disinfection enacted in your presence,
cry out for the chambermaid.

Colombo, Sri Lanka:

Please do not bathe outside the bathtub.

Switzerland:

It is defended to promenade the corridors in the boots of the mountain in front of six hours.

Copenhagen, Denmark:

Take care of burglars.

Italy:

Please report all leakings on the part of the staff.

Hue, Vietnam:

Toilet was cleaned and spayed.

Austria:

Not to perambulate the corridors in the hours
of repose in the boots of ascension.

Athens, Greece:

Visitors are expected to complain at the office
between the hours of 9 and 11 a.m. daily.

Moscow, Russia:

If this is your first visit to the USSR,
you are welcome to it.

Japan:

Cooles and Heates:

If you want just condition of warm in your room,
please control yourself.

Acapulco, Mexico:

The manager has personally passed
all the water served here.

Hotel rate card in Chiang Mai, Thailand:

Extra Bad – 150 baht.

Brasov, Romania:

Dear Guts.

Serbia:

The flattening of underwear with pleasure
is the job of the chambermaid.
Turn to her straightaway.

Mexico City:

We sorry to advise you that by a electric disperfect
in the generator master of the elevator we have
the necessity that don't give service at our
distinguishable guests.

Moscow:

The passenger must get free the room before
two o'clocks of the day they are abandoning in other
case, as the passenger fracture the day and must
the administration pay for full.

Zurich:

Do you wish to change in Zurich?
Do so at the hotel bank!

Italy:

Do not adjust yor light hanger.
If you wish more light see manager.

Japan:

Depositing the room key into another person
is prohibited.

Lobby shop in Kuantan, Malaysia:

Found in the lobby.

Japan:

Please to bathe inside the tub.

Taiwan:

Do not wear slippers to prevent falling in bath.

Thailand:

Please do not bring solicitors into your room.

Gaspe Peninsula, Canada:

No dancing in the bathrooms!

Tokyo:

Keep your hands away from unnecessary buttons
for you.

Rio de Janeiro, Brazil:

Visit the hairdresser in the Sub Soil of this Hotel.

France:

Wondering what to wear? A sports jacket
may be worn to dinner, but no trousers.

Japan:

You are invited to take advantage
of the chambermaid.

Hotel on the Ionian Sea:

In order to prevent shoes from mislaying, please don't
corridor them. The management cannot be held.

Palma de Mallorca, Majorca:

Every Sunday very greay kocks fights at Ca'n Veta jurt in front of the ancient rase horces.

Guest questionnaire from a hotel in Lavenham, Suffolk, UK:

Was there a particular member of staff who made you stay memorable?

Guest questionnaire, Vinales, Cuba:

1. What did you look for?

2. What did you find it?

Possible 'How was the service?' answers:

A. Excellent

B. The awaited one

C. Almost the awaiting one

D. Nothing

Poland:

Sweat dreams.

Zurich:

Because of the impropriety of entertaining guests
of the opposite sex in the bedroom, it is suggested
that the lobby be used for this purpose.

Beijing:

No permission to wench.

---

*You'd think that if there was one thing on which hotels
would make themselves clear, it'd be their fire procedure.
Think again . . .*

Finland:

If you cannot reach a fire exit, close the door
and expose yourself at the window.

Florence, Italy:

Fire! It is what we can be doing, we hope.
No fear. Not ourselves. Say quickly to all people
coming up down, everywhere, a prayer always
is a clerk. He is assured of safety by expert men
who are in the bar for telephone for the fighters
of the fire come out.

Milan:

In case of a fire in your room
and your inability to put the fire out:
Leave the room closing the door,
find the exit following the signals.
Don't bother with your luggage.
Don't use the elevators (lifts).
Don't shout or run. Try to inform the desk,
any personnel you might get across.

France:

In the event of fire the visitor, avoiding panic,
is to walk down the corridor to warn
the chambermaid.

Moscow:

By all means report the fire to the floor-attendant
or to any other authority of the hotel.

Copenhagen:

In the event of fire, open a window and announce
your presence in a seemly manner.

Beijing:

No smoking in bed.
If it's on fire the guests should be disperse
according to the safety way.

Vienna, Austria:

In case of fire, do your utmost to alarm
the hotel porter.

Saudi Arabia:

In case of fire, please read this.

Japan:

In case of fire,
try to use the fire ex-ting wisher.

London, UK:

All fire extinguishers must be examined
at least five days before any fire.

*Laon, France, English translation of a sign
in French, reading* 'En cas de feu – restez calme':

In case of fire do not lose your temper.

*Sometimes it's even more serious
than fire . . .*

Tokyo:

In case of earthquake,
use the torch to pass yourself out.

*Feeling peckish? Why not pop down
to your friendly hotel restaurant? . . .*

Madrid:

Our wine list leaves you nothing to hope for.

Belgrade:

Restauroom open daily.

Torremolinos:

We highly recommend the hotel tart.

Ho Chi Minh City, Vietnam:

Tasty tacos and beautiful tarts
are the order of the day.

Vietnam:

Compulsory Buffet Breakfast.

Jakarta, Indonesia:

Wondering where to eat?
Grill and roast your clients!
Open for lunch,
dinner and Sunday brunch.

Nairobi, Kenya:

Customers who find our waitresses rude
ought to see the manager.

Bulgaria:

If you are satisfactory, tell your friends.
If you are unsatisfactory, warn the waitress.

Poland:

As for the tripe served you at the Hotel Monopol,
you will be singing its praises
to your grandchildren on your deathbed.

Sri Lanka:

A La Crate Menu.

Ankara:

You are invite to visit our restaurant
where you can eat the Middle East Foods
in a European ambulance.

Miyanoshita, Japan:

We now have a Sukiyaki Restaurant
with lodging facilities for those who want
to have experiences on Japanese bedding.

Jakarta:

JP Bistro – a contemporary brassiere-style
restaurant . . .

*Of course, competition in the hotel industry is fierce.
Owners will do anything to get your business.
Anything, that is, except check what they've written . . .*

Sicilian travel brochure:

Bath in room, pavements in cooked.

*Replies from German hotels in response to enquiries
about accommodation:*

We have ample garage accommodation
for your char.

In the close village you can buy jolly memorials
for when you pass away.

I send you my prices. If I am dear to you and
your mistress she might perhaps be reduced.

We are also noted for having children.

I am honourable to accept your impossible request.
Unhappy it is I here have not bedroom with bath.
A bathroom with bed I have. I can though give you
a washing with pleasure in a most clean spring with no
person to see. I insist that you will like this.

I am amazing diverted by your entreaty for a room.
I can offer you a commodious chamber with a balcony
imminent to the romantic gorge and I hope you will
want to drop in.

A vivacious stream washes my doorsteps so do not
concern yourself that I am not too good in bath.
I am superb in bed.

Sorrowfully I cannot abide your auto.

Having freshly taken over the proprietry of this
notorious house, I am wishful that you remove to me
your esteemed costume.

Standing among savage scenery the hotel offers
stupendous revelations. There is a French widow in
every bedroom, affording delightful prospects.

I give personal look to the interior wants
of each guest. Here you shall be well fed up,
and agreeably drunk.

Our charges for weekly visitors are scarcely creditable.

Peculiar arrangements for gross parties.

Our motto is 'ever serve you right'.

A hotel should be a home from home. But then again,
it's at home where most deaths occur.

Assistant public relations manager of a Jakarta hotel
after a death there (reported in the Jakarta Post*):*

Please tell the public not to kill themselves on hotel
property if they want to die. It only confounds us.
They can do it in the river for example.

Advert for a Tokyo hotel:

Our staffs are always here waiting for you
to patronize them.

Hotel brochure in Qingdao, China:

Hua Tian Hotel is among the few best
foreign affairs hotels.

Hotel in Sorrento:

Syrene Bellevue Hotel joins a modern functional
equipment with a distinguished and smart style
of the 18th century. The restaurant salon with a large
view of the Gulf of Naples, a restaurant service with
a big choice, the private beach to be reached by a lift
from inside directly, complete the undiscussable
peculiarities of this unit.

Driven to Distraction

*One of the easiest ways to get lost in translation
is by car . . .*

Japanese road sign:

Stop. Drive sideways.

Sign in a hire car, Tokyo, Japan:

When passenger of foot heave in sight, tootle
the horn. Trumpet him melodiously at first,
but if he still obstacles your passage
then tootle him with vigor.

Outside a shop in Athens, Greece:

Park one hour. Later dick dock goes
the money clock.

Sign in Tokyo:

Cars will not have intercourse
on this bridge.

And another:

Try bigger and bigger
but keep more and more slowly.

'Dead end' road sign, Istanbul, Turkey:

No more. Please pack up now.

Sign in Beijing, China,
warning of dangerous road surface:

To take notice of safe,
the slippery are very crafty.

Instructions on Japanese driving rules:

At the rise of the hand of the policeman, stop rapidly.
Do not pass him, otherwise disrespect him.
Do not explosion the exhaust pipe.
Avoid entanglement with your wheel spoke.
Go soothingly on the grease mud
as there lurks a skid demon.

From owner's manual of Toyota car:

Please not to listen to cassette
while the radio is talking.

Road signs in India:

Avoid Overspeeding.

Always Avoid Accidents.

Luxor, Egypt:

Parking in wrong places will make you accountalbe
to law apart from being a trespassing on the right
of the citizen and the state.

Traffic sign, Karachi, Pakistan:

Please avoid accidents here.

Notice at a Tokyo immigration office:

**Do not use parking lot as we expect
a great deal of dustle.**

In a Japanese taxi:

Safety first.

Please put on your seatbelt.

Prepare for accident.

Sign on a car in Manila, Philippines:

Car and owner for sale.

Japanese brochure:

**Toyota E-com will be come a main type of car
suitable for commutation in metropolis
and the suburbs nearly in the future.**

Sign at a car repair shop in Bali, Indonesia:
Cat Oven.

Solvent sold in Finland for unfreezing car locks:
Super piss.

Petrol station, Santa Fe, New Mexico:
We will sell gasoline to anyone in a glass container.

At a motoring event on the French Riviera:
Competitors will defile themselves on the promenade at 11 a.m., and each car will have two drivers who will relieve themselves at each other's convenience.

On a Japanese car engine:
The ARC Product is wonders assenbiled project. They present comfortable and unknown car life with ARC power.

On the spare wheel cover of a Japanese 4×4:

It's an outdoor sport that has recently started to shine.
Outdoor sport is the science to raise spirits.
To choose sports for fashion or your personality.
The basic idea is to enjoy yourself.
That is important.

Another:

Nissan Terrano is for the car enthusiast who wants
to feel the beat of life in his own life.

Yet another:

Whenever and everywhere, we can meet our best
friend – nature. Take a grip of steering!

On the front of a Japanese lorry:

Challenge safe driving for the 21st century.

Sticker on the windscreen of Japanese sports car:

OFFRIMITS

On the side of a Japanese van:

We think that we want to contribute to society through daiamond drilling and wire sawing.

And on another:

Brain Location Service.

Advert for a Japanese car:

Exciting Pleasure World accessories.

Style up Performa.

Notice on the windscreen of a van in London's Chinatown:

Driver on derivery.

Norwegian TV host to an American guest who complained about the slippery winter roads:

But didn't you have pigs in your decks?

A Healthy Respect
for Language

If you ain't got your health, you ain't got nothin'.
But if you get lost in translation, you've got even less . . .

In a maternity ward in Pumwani, Kenya:
No children allowed.

In a hospital in Barcelona, Spain:
Visitors two to a bed and half an hour only.

On a Japanese medicine bottle:
Adults: 1 tablet 3 times a day until passing away.

Advertisement for a Hong Kong dentist:
Teeth extracted by the latest Methodists.

Turkish bath in Rome:

Be pleased to come lie down with our masseuse.
She will make you forget all your tired.

From a Japanese medical questionnaire:

Are you haunted by horribles?
Do you ever run after your nose?

Does your nose choke?
Does your head or face or shoulder ever limp?
Has any part of your body suddenly grown
uncontrollable?

Advisory booklet for expectant mothers,
Public Health Centre, Joetsu City, Japan:

1. Strain yourself or push at the time of contraction and two hours later a baby will come out.

2. A swell will be checked if there is, by pushing shin.

3. If your weight gains rapidly, it is a sign of swell or fatness.

4. If you pick up around your nipple come out 1 cm high, and it'll be alright.

5. You'd better begin your sexual intercourse after the delivery after the one mouth check-up with a doctor.

6. If you want to do a vowel movement don't stop.

7. After you vomit, you rinse your mouse and if you can eat, eat.

8. You can do ãfoo, fooä naturally when you open your mouth slightly.

9. Brasure can be for maternity one or nursing bra, so that your breast can't be oppressed.

10. There are many differences of ideas in family but she felt family bondage after delivery as a wife.

On Chinese medicine bottle:

Known to cure itching, colds, stomachs, brains, and other diseases.

On another Chinese medicine bottle:

Expiration date: 2 years.

Newspaper advertisement, Manila, Philippines:

It's Summer Time!
Bring your children to the Garma Specialty Clinic for Circumcision. (Children and Adult). Painless. Bloodless. German cut.

Swedish parents explaining to an American doctor that their daughters' thighs are bruised from a clapping game:

The girls have blue pricks.

In the office of a doctor in Rome, Italy:

Specialist in women and other diseases.

Sri Lanka:

Sanitary Napking Disposal Bag.

Massage offered at a hotel in Kandy, Sri Lanka:

Body massage is done synchronously,
to prevent parts of the body
getting over activated.

And their nasal massage:

After the treatment you will feel very clean
and more clear nostrils.

It's not just a case of feeling good —
you've got to look your best too . . .

Barbershop in Tokyo, Japan:

All customers promptly executed.

Barbershop in Zanzibar, Tanzania:

Gentlemen's throats cut
with nice sharp razors.

On a Taiwanese shampoo:

Use repeatedly for severe damage.

German skin cream:

Cream Shower for pretentious skin.

Beauty shop in Chuo Rinkan, Japan:

Beauty Brain's Fantastic Fannie.

Herbalist's catalogue in Venice, Italy:

Make Thin! Obesity is a well known trouble.
Fat people must not take around a majestic fatness,
wearing large suits, perspirating too much.

Diet centre in Poughkeepsie, New York, USA:

Lose all your weight: $198.

Japanese public bath:

Foreign guests are requested not to pull cock in tub.

Beijing, China:

Haircuts half price today.
Only one per customer.

Jeweller's window, India:

We shoot earholes.

Eating Your Words

*Food is a universal language. We all share a need for it,
an enjoyment of it, a fascination with it. Pity we ruin
everything by making such a pig's ear of describing it . . .*

Europe:

Boiled Frogfish.

On a Polish menu:

Salad a firm's own make; limpid red beet soup
with cheesy dumplings in the form of a finger;
roasted duck let loose; beef rashers beaten up
in the country people's fashion.

Cambodian menu:

Fried internal part of chicken with mushrooms
and deep fried fist with vegetables.

China:

Cold shredded children
and sea blubber
in spicy sauce.

Los Angeles, USA:

French creeps.

Vienna, Austria:

Fried milk, children sandwiches,
roast cattle and boiled sheep.

*Translation of 'paté de maison'
on a Calais, France, menu:*

Our pie.

Yalta, Ukraine:

Climbing with a hen.

Europe:

Sole Bonne Femme
(Fish Landlady style).

Akko, Israel:

Lamp chops.

Hong Kong:

Indonesian Nazi Goreng.

Cairo, Egypt:

Muscles of marines / Lobster thermos.

Japan:

Buttered saucepans and fried hormones.

China:

Dreaded veal cutlet with potatoes in cream.

Hong Kong:

Rainbow trout, fillet streak, popotoes,
chocolate mouse.

Cairo:

Prawn cock and tail.

Vietnam:

Pork with fresh garbage.

Japan:

Fried fishermen.

India:

Deep fried fingers of my lady.

Spain:

Goose barnacles.

Cairo:

French fried ships.

Japan:

Teppan yaki – before your cooked right eyes.

Costa Rica:

Jam and cheese sandwich.

India:

Children soup.

Barcelona, Spain:

Grilled lamp ribs.

Bali, Indonesia:

Toes with butter and jam.

Cairo:

Cock in wine / Lioness cutlet.

Brazil:

Vegitational beef soap.

Barcelona:

'Boys style' little chickens.

Nepal:

Fried friendship.

Laos:

Friend eggs.

Chinese buffet in Canada:

Cram Chowder.

Poland:

Chessburger.

Poland:

Hod dok.

Singapore:

Sir Loin steak with potato cheeps.

Macao:

Utmost of chicken fried in bother.

Menu in France offering egg:

An extract of fowl, peached or sunside up.

Venezuela:

Fried chicken babies, fungus cream
and grill cattle bowels.

Tarragona, Spain:

Take Hawai salads.

Mexico:

Grilled Potties.

Egypt:

Hot dog mustache pringle.

*Goat, as presented by a restaurant
on the Greek island of Antiparos:*

Kid baked in clay flowerpot.

Thailand:

Chicken gordon blue, pork shops,
eggs scrambling.

Indonesia:

Cajun chicken biceps.

Algericas, Spain:

Revolting eggs.

*Soups of the day,
Chinese restaurant in the USA:*

Ckicken velvet and ckicken noddle.

Nepal:

Complimentary glass wine or bear.

Billboard in Delhi:

Hamburgers, pizzas, ice cream and snakes.

France:

Nut of Holy Jacques jumped, guinea fowl stinks
to it and its farce with cheese-topped dish, almost
cheese-dish of mould in spice on bed of spinach.

Slovakia:

Hamanegs.

Thailand:

Rather burnt land slug.

Shanghai, China:

Our Mongolean hot pot buffet guarantees
you will be able to eat all you wish
until you are fed up.

*French restaurant in Hong Kong,
under 'cheeses':*

Roguefart.

*Thai restaurant in Toronto, Canada,
indicating the spiciest dish available:*

Flames to the whole boyd.

Chinese restaurant in London, UK:

Assorted Meat Fried Noodle

With Meat £2.70

With Named Meat £3.50

With Other Meat £4.60

Canberra, Australia:

Dumping soup.

Thailand:

Curly flower.

General Chaos Chicken.

We are also have fun food you are never had before.

We are always look for new food.

Thank you for eating our delicious food.

We will never stop creating your tasted food.

Steamed fillet of new zeal and orange roughy.

Quality kept foods warm.

Fresh thousand year old eggs.

Riga, Latvia:

Salad: cucumber, salad sheets,
mayonnaise, ovum.

Spicy dish at a Chinese restaurant in Memphis, USA:

. . . will make you cry silently.

Japan:

Sexy calamari leg.

*Restaurant in San Juan, Puerto Rico,
serving crab and conch:*

Grab and crunch.

China:

Mr Zheng and his fellow workers like to meet you
and entertain you with hostility and unique
cooking technique.

Chinese restaurant in Toronto,
describing boneless chicken:

Bong lens chicken.

From Japanese menus:

Savour best match of the mysterious sauces.

Modernly arranged miscellaneous European Flavors.

Vietnam bird salad, mixed Chimaki and asian corses.

Seasonal ingredients specially pre-pared and directly
imported from their place of origination.

Kansas City, USA:

Ho-made Chili.

Indian restaurant in Grantham, UK:

Brinjal bhaji (Aborigine).

Café in Smithfield Market, London:

Chinese fried noddle.

Café in the Empire State Building, New York:
All our eggs made with 3 omeletes.

Café just off Oxford Street, London:
Jacket potato with mixed vegetable cause.

And, as one of its sandwich fillings:
smocked salmon.

Athens, Greece:
Chopped cow with a wire through it
and bowels in sauce.

Greek menu:
Spleen omelet, fisherman's crap soup,
calf pluck, bowels.

Café in London:
Jacked potatoes.

Restaurant in London (for 'biryanis'):

Bryanies.

And for dessert . . .

Japan:

Strawberry crap.

Europe:

Sweat from the trolley.

China, describing a pancake dish:

Waiter will roll in front of you.

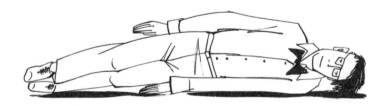

Costa Rica:

Pastry Chef.

Thailand:

Waffies.

---

*Would you like anything to drink
with that? . . .*

Europe:

Garlic coffee.

Ingolstadt, Germany:

Coffee and snakes.

India:

**Our establishment serves tea
in a bag like mother.**

Indian restaurant in London:

WINE LIST

Larger

Carlsberg – Pint

---

*That's just the food itself –
service is not included . . .*

Malaysia:

Seafood brought in by customers
will not be entertained.

Tokyo, Japan:

Please do not bring outside food
excluding children under five.

Paris, France:

We serve five o'clock tea
at all hours.

India:

After one visit we guarantee you will be regular.

Italy:

Please pay the house waiter the price
of your consummation.

Hong Kong:

Come broil yourself at your open table.

Neon sign outside a restaurant in China:

Smart noshery makes u slobber.

Swiss mountain inn:

Special today – no ice cream.

Restaurant in the Swiss Alps:

No skies inside.

*Menu in a river-boat restaurant, Thailand,
informs diners that if they bring their own drinks...*

they will be charged 400 baht cockage.

*Sign outside a restaurant, Chiang Mai,
Thailand, announces that it's now...*

contemporary closed.

Michigan, USA:

The early bird gets the worm!
Special shoppers' luncheon before 11 a.m.

*In the bathroom of a Chinese restaurant,
Detroit, USA:*

Employees must wash your hands..

Chelsea, London:

Plat du jour, changed each day.

Mumbai, India:

Seven days a week and weekends too.

*Japanese restaurant in Oceanside,
California, USA:*

Test our pride.

Tokyo restaurant advertisement:

Colorful dining space
surrounded by stained glasses.

Sign in a Chinese restaurant, USA:

WARNING: Tips for waitress not privilege
off customer, and not optonal to do! Is custimarry
and IS THE LAW for leave tips, otherwise is possibul
to face prostection by law! Please be responsivele,
leave tip and no go jail! Have a nice day!

Sign in a London pizza restaurant:

Open 24 hours except 2 a.m.–8 a.m.

Thailand:

For our convenience,
we do not accept checks.

*On one Chinese menu, various dishes are marked with
an asterisk. At the bottom of the page, it states . . .*

the asterisk means handicapped accessible.

In the bathroom of the same restaurant:

With deepest respect,
we hope to wish our insistence
you washes your hands when using our facility.

Vietnamese restaurant in USA:

Troublemakers will be Bard!

Have Nice Day.

We will be honouring your delivering
in the fast time as possible.

No surrender!
Eat as much as your tummy can challenge!

Chinese restaurant in Charlotte,
North Carolina, USA:

No MSG. We care you health.

Chinese restaurant in Brooklyn, New York:

Fast free delivery by the cars.

Sign on the door of an Italian restaurant,
Osaka, Japan:

Hospitality now, or in 10 minutes.

Korean restaurant in Auckland, New Zealand:

We do not re-use the food.

Various Chinese restaurants in the USA:

We can alter the spicy according to your wishes.

We delivery ahead.

Lunch Buffet $4.99

Chicken 3–8 years old $2.95

Indian restaurant in London's Mayfair:

We are established since 1963.
Our first restaurant was arranged to be open
on Saturday 23rd November – the same day
as the Kennedy assassination happened.
[It was actually the 22nd.] It was a loss of a very
important person all over the world.

When it comes to Chinese food,
sometimes the name of the restaurant says it all . . .

Kuala Lumpur, Malaysia:

Soon Go Fatt.

Baltimore, USA:

Eat Must Be First.

Pittsburgh, USA:

My Dung.

Night-Time
is the Right Time

*You're wined and dined – now you want a night
on the town. Trouble is, the town isn't making
things all that clear . . .*

Cairo, Egypt:

**Unaccompanied ladies not admitted
unless with husband or similar.**

Shanghai, China:

Restaurant and bra.

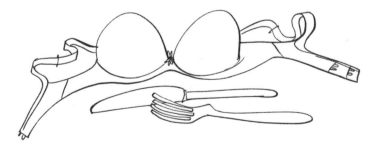

Sign outside a Mexican disco:
Members and non-members only.

Advertisement for a disco, Luxembourg:
Let's fun.

Sign outside a Mexican bar:
Sorry, we're open!

In a bar in Tokyo, Japan:
Special cocktails for the ladies with nuts.

Caption from the Soviet Union,
under a picture of a dance evening:
Young men's balls in full swing.

Sign outside a bar in Bangkok, Thailand:
The shadiest cocktail bar in town.

Norway:

Ladies are requested not to have children
in the bar.

*From a brochure for a supper club at Ambassador City
Jomtien resort, Pattaya, Thailand:*

Relieve yourself in an ideal of karaoke
and live music in bewitching time.

*Of course, you could always set your cultural
sights a little higher . . .*

Italy:
*Genoa Opera Company's
description of* Carmen, *Act IV:*

A place in Seville. Procession of Ball-fighters.
The roaring of balls is heard in the arena. Aria and
chorus: 'Toreador, Toreador. All hail the Balls of a
toreador.' Enter Don Jose singing, 'I besmooch you.'
Carmen repels him. He stabbs her.
Aria: 'Oh, rupture, rupture.'

Notice at Bolshoi Theatre, Moscow, Russia:

We ask to excuse for the possible caused inconveniences in connection with work on reconstruction of theatre.

Tested to Instruction

The modern world is a stressful place. But don't worry, there are countless gadgets and devices on hand to make life easier. Just remember the golden rule when operating them: never read the instructions first . . .

Hong Kong alarm clock:

To set alarm set alarm hand to time desired to wake. To change time desired to wake, reset alarm to the time desired to.

Swedish flat-packed cabinet:

It is advisory to be 2 people during assembly.

Japanese haemorrhoid treatment:

Lie down on bed and insert product slowly up to the projected portion like a sword-guard into anal duct. while inserting product for approximatly 5 minuites, keep quiet.

*Telus LG1000, a Korean mobile phone
aimed at ages eight to twelve:*

Open-minded: Easy-to-use in Structure.

Getting along with you, I reveal my secret
to you, buddy.

Despite such strengths listed above,
I need enough food to get energy.

For you to see me, get to know me more
and hang out with me longer.

My favorite food is battery!

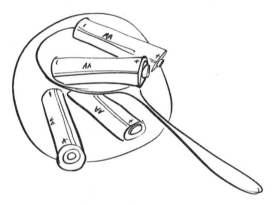

When I am tired, please give my words
to your parents to energize me.
Or I have to go to bed without seeing you.

Let's not make a scene when we meet
not to disturb others especially in class or library.

Leaflet found by a householder:

The washers contained into the kit must be absolutely assembled also when the manifold is without them.

The householder couldn't remember – or imagine – which appliance the leaflet came with.

The Chinese company Xue Sheng Xi Lie Zhi Chi's safety guide for its 18-cm ruler:

This product was easy to burning, aloof the high temperature, please. Because maybe beget any danger and the product's definition distort.
The product have some keenness part, so need to prevent bruise. The product only befit measure and study, unable to do other definition's measure. Needed the pater-familias accompany, if the children haven't 3 years.

Chinese headset magnifying glass:

Maintance: This product is made of acrylic. So don't rub by chemical medicine to avoid lens spoiled. Just use medium alcohol to rub it lightly. Watch carefully for use.

MP3 player:

Pause now you are in shortly, stop.

Taiwanese spanner:

Easy to use, it is only a simple Ratchet-Action.
The more tension. The more steady,
while in operation.

Chinese red warning light:

Suitable for bi cycle, jogging, climbing,
baby-car, disable-car. Especially for the children,
blind men, old men, in the morning or evening,
and the cloudy day, when the bright is not enough,
to increase more safety.

Chinese travel clock:

Attention before you use it. 1. Please pull out
the PVC insulation sheet Beside the battery-cover
on the bottom, Then the Music will come up.
Press any Key to stop it. This is regular situation.

Chinese candle:

Keep this candle out of children.

Chinese scooter:

Safe drive notice to the motorcycle drivers.
There is the condition for you to drive a motorcycle
Safely and make it serve to you faithfully The
condition is to keep the safety in your mind forever.

Taiwanese room spray:

Can be used at any place where needs to eliminate the
stinky smell and keep fleshing surroundings at all time.

Chinese bath sponge:

Pull with your hands and stick it on your body,
you will feel great as bathing.

Taiwanese puzzle toy:

Let's decompose and enjoy assembling!

*Chinese model kit, stating that paint and glue
are not included:*

This kit cannot be completed with paint and glue.

Chinese toy:

Avoid disturbing the other while enjoying this item.

During cutting, do not put your head too close.

There is difference between up and down.

Beware of being swallowed by child,
due to small parts.

On a Chinese toy boat:

Please don't place it in following place:
(a) nearby strong vibration. (b) in the dusty play.

Taiwanese wading boots:

Warning! Difficult to swim out if wearing wader
filled with water by falling down! Therefor,
please avoid deep water where danger
of drowning possibility exists.

Pack of toy animals sold in Ranong, Thailand:

Be careful of being eaten by small children.

Japanese phone card:

1. Lift up receiver. 2. Insert phone card.
3. Dial 0999 + number. 4. Say Hello.

Japanese radio:

You will know radio on by enchanting green light.

Japanese telephone:

Plug the phone jack into the wall. If the phone rings,
pick it up and greet the person on the other end
by saying 'Hello!' or another such greeting.
Once completing your conversation,
hang up the phone.

Chinese computer monitor:

Please be sure to keep the vents on top open.
Do not bring spillables near these,
like chicken soup and dust.

Phone in Japanese hotel:

For long distance Dial 0 and Aria Cord.

Cashpoint screen, Taiwan:

When operating the Automatic Teller Machine
(ATM), you should keep attention on the screen.
Do not believe any indications that you can operate
the ATM with a cell phone, telephone, or leaflets.

Greek deodorant stick:

Push up bottom.

Japanese washing machine:

Push button.
Foam coming plenty.
Big noise.
Finish.

Instructions with Chinese exercise balls:

Three types of ball are offered.
They are one. two. three.

---

*Sometimes, there's an awful lot to be said
for the straightforward approach . . .*

*On a fire extinguisher,
Calcutta (Kolkata), India:*

Cease Fire.

Transport Trouble

It's often said that travel broadens the mind.
It seems to do the opposite for the vocabulary . . .

On a ferry from Tenerife to La Gomera, Canary Islands:
Keep this ticket up the end of your trip.

Sign on underground, in Shanghai, China,
informing passengers that the way out is up the stairs:
Exit – make-up.

Notice in a sleeping carriage on Indian train:
Do not invite thieves to sleep in the floor.

On a Japanese tourist map:
Shitseeing Bus Stop.

Sign onboard ship in Mobile, Alabama, USA:

Warning: despite our best efforts, park exhibits slip,
fall, head strike, cut, pinch, ankle twist, spray paint
mist, particle breathing, alligator bite, heat lightning,
and stress risks – particularly to unsupervised children,
rambunctious youths and over exerted adults.

On a Vietnamese boat:

Nobody is allowed to sit on the both sides of the boat.

On a Soviet ship in the Black Sea:

Helpsavering apparata in emergings behold
many whistles! Associate the stringing apparata
about the bosoms and meet behind. Flee then
to the indifferent lifesavering shippen obediencing
the instructs of the vessel chef.

Ferry in San Juan, Puerto Rico, harbour:

In case of emergency,
the lifeguards are under the seat
in the center of the vessel.

Beijing, China:

Danger prohibited aboard this boat.

Indonesian travel brochure:

If we are lucky we will see duck boys home,
men massaging their cocks on the road, cow boys
taking grass. Yes it is a wonderful experience.

In a travel agency in Barcelona, Spain:

Go away.

Caption for a photo, in a Japanese magazine,
of a London Routemaster bus:

Double dicker.

Sign at the ferry terminal in Davao, Philippines:

Adults: 1 USD
Child: 50 cents
Cadavers: subject to negotiation.

Venezuelan travel brochure:

In this Expedition you will know the highets waterfall in the world. From Canaima, through the Sabana, the Jungles and the rivers Carrao and Churun, you'll enjoy one of the biggets emotions of this life. And the facilities Camp. Guides as natives, all experts, will bring you trough troubles waters, just where a few have made it. Be you one of them. Meals in open fire never taste so goo.

French tourist brochure:

In France, you can cruise on many canals and see the peculiarities.

Let Me Entertain You

The beauty of getting lost in translation is that entertainment can entertain even when it doesn't. Never mind that the film's predictable, the song's unlistenable, the computer game's tedious. There's still hope – they might have got some of the words wrong . . .

Videos available in Hong Kong:

Fargo: Mysterious Murder in Snowy Cream

The Full Monty: Six Stripped Warriors

The English Patient: Don't Ask Me Who I Am

Boogie Nights: His Powerful Device Makes Him Famous

Nixon: The Big Liar

The Professional: This Hit Man Is Not As Cold As He Thought

Good Will Hunting: Bright Sun, Just Like Me

Dead Poets Society: Bright Sun In Heavy Rain

As Good As It Gets: Mr. Cat Poop

Pirated videos in Suriname:

Deep Throat: Deep Trout

Death On The Nile: Dead On The Nail

Advertisements for films being shown in Taiwan:

Six Days, Seven Nights: After *Air Force One*, Harrison Ford is flying a airplane, again!

Small Soldiers: The style of characters is phat, special effects are cool, this film is phat and cool.

The Avengers: The perfect style with a great taste to save the world.

English subtitles from films available in Hong Kong:

Same old rules: no eyes, no groin.

I have been scared shitless too much lately.

This will be of fine service for you, you bag of the scum. I am sure you will not mind that I remove your manhoods and leave them out on the dessert floor for your aunts to eat.

Yah-hah, evil spider woman! I have captured you by the short rabbits and can now deliver you violently to your gynecologist for a thorough extermination.

Greetings, large black person. Let us not forget to form a team up together and go into the country to inflict the pain of our karate feets on some ass of the giant lizard person.

The Iceman Cometh: I threat you! I challenge you meet me on the roof tonight for a duet!

I will kill you until you are dead from it!

Fong Sai-Yuk II: He started it first!

The Kung Fu Cult Master: Just scold Chang as 'Shame-less asshole' for three times. Then you will free from this kind of suffer forever.

You will not happy ending!

The Kung Fu Cult Master: Master, where are those
people of Ming Sect? They seem to be disappeared.

Once Upon a Time in China and America:
I've to cut partial of my freedom.

Dr Wai and the Scripture Without Words:
He is jealousing!

It is destinated to be you!

Lethal Panther: The bullets inside are very hot.
Why do I feel so cold?

As Tears Go By: I got knife-scars more than the
number of your leg's hair!

Holy Weapon: I am damn unsatisfied to be killed
in this way.

Pedicab Driver: Fatty, you with your thick face
have hurt my instep.

Pom Pom and Hot Hot: I'll fire aimlessly
if you don't come out!

You are too useless. And now I must beat you.

Rich and Famous: Gun wounds again?

Brain Theft: A normal person wouldn't steal pituitaries.

Pedicab Driver: You always use violence.
I should've ordered glutinous rice chicken.

The Seventh Curse: Take my advice,
or I'll spank you without pants.

Saviour of the Soul:
Beware! Your bones are going to be disconnected.

Police Story 2: Beat him out of recognizable shape!

Armour of God:
Who gave you the nerve to get killed here?

The Beheaded 100:
How can you use my intestines as a gift?

On the Run: Quiet or I'll blow your throat up.

Satyr Monks: You daring lousy guy.

Pedicab Driver:
Damn, I'll burn you into a BBQ chicken!

Quotes from Western films shown in Japan:

Forrest Gump, for 'My momma always said life was like
a box of chocolates. You never know what you're
gonna get': 'The life where Mama was said always
seemed like the box of the chocolate. The profit
which does not know those which are gonna
under any condition do.'

Dirty Harry, for 'You've got to ask yourself a question:
"Do I feel lucky?" Well, do ya, punk?':
'It asks 1 in you yourself, it becomes: "As for me
fortunately is felt?" To be good, as for ya and punk?'

Casablanca, for 'Of all the gin joints in all the towns
in all the world, she walks into mine': 'In all towns
of the all worlds of all gin, her it connects to
my ones which you walk.'

*Tag line on a Chinese DVD copy
of* The Matrix Revolutions*:*

**The White Men
Wanted A Stud To Breed Slaves.**

*It's not just movies
where things go wrong . . .*

Japanese copy of a Meatloaf album includes the tracks:

'You Took The Words Right Out Of My Mouse'
and (for **'Two Out Of Three Ain't Bad'**)
'Sixty Six Per Cent Is All Right'.

Bootleg CD available in China:

Seargent Peeper's Lonely Hearts Club Band.

And, by the same band:

'Hey Tube'.

On an Indonesian bootleg U2 album:

'Angle of Harlem'.

Caption in a Japanese magazine next to picture of famous actor:

Jude Low.

And That's Official

They can lock you up, take your money and ask you lots of impertinent questions. So it's nice to know that when it comes to language, the powers that be sometimes have powers that aren't . . .

Vietnamese customs form:

Objects must be declared.
If there isn't any object mark X only
at the quantity Yes column and
if there are any objects, cross out
letter No and at the same row write
exact amount of weight of these objects
in words or in figures.

Same form forbids:

Giving false declaration
or having the action of tricking.

Letter sent by Rotterdam police:

You did not report yourself by the Alien police.
You have to do this in a short time, otherwise
you get troubles! When you don't come
to our office, we demand you to come!
And when you don't come again, you maybe
have to pay a fine, and it is possible
that you will be expanded.

On a Hungarian visa form:

Your answers should be typewritten
or printed in case of handwriting.

Recorded information line, Australia
(set up to answer questions about the new Goods
and Services tax plan):

If you understand English, press 1.
If you do not understand English, press 2.

From a meeting in the European Commission:

The chairman called the meeting to order
and asked if there were any matters
to discuss under the table.

Shop Soiled

*The first rule of retail is that the customer
is always right. The second seems to be that
the grammar is always wrong . . .*

In a Majorcan shop:

English well talking here speeching American.

In an Israeli butcher's:

I slaughter myself twice daily.

Shop in Budapest, Hungary:

Very smart! Almost pansy!

Shop sign on Lovina Beach in Bali, Indonesia:

Feel like shopping? We have no good things to sell.

Grocer's shop, Japan:
Flesh Food.

Sign outside Chinese store:
We try our best to decrease your life.

Name of shop in Medan, Indonesia:
68% Perfect Shop.

Notice in a dry-cleaner's window in Bangkok, Thailand:
Drop your trousers here for the best results.

Clothes shop in Paris, France:
Dresses for street walking.

Laundry in Rome, Italy:
Ladies, leave your clothes here
and spend the afternoon having a good time.

Sign over a pet store in Osaka, Japan:
Fondle dogs.

Store in Amman, Jordan:
Visit our bargain basement – one flight up.

In the same store they sell:
Pork Handbags.

Swedish furrier:
Fur coats made for ladies from their own skin.

Outside a tailor's in Hong Kong:
Ladies may have a fit upstairs.

Shop in Tokyo, Japan:
Our nylons cost more than common,
but you'll find they are best in the long run.

On a Japanese shopping bag:
Now baby.
Tonight I am feeling cool
and hard boiled.

On another:
Switzerland: seaside city.

Advertisement for a Tokyo antique shop:
This shop has been moved to the present place
for 35 years.

Tailor in Rhodes, Greece:

Order your summers suit. Because is big rush,
we will execute customers in strict rotation.

Sign in a shop on the island of Cozumel, near Mexico:

Broken English Spoken Perfectly.

*Notice on a soup terrine in a German
cash-and-carry store:*

Pie Soup.

*Chiselled in the marble façade
of a Japanese clothing shop:*

Dresses for ladies and gentlemen.

At a Hong Kong costume shop:

This merchandise is to be used
for turning a trick on Halloween.

Turkish shop:

All peoples welcome for the gifts.

Clothes shop in Brussels, Belgium:

Mourning and sportswear.

Gift shop in Nice, France:

Our police:
no return, no exchange.

Sign in a Hong Kong supermarket:

For your convenience,
we recommend coitus,
efficient self-service.

*Shop in Shanghai, China,
aiming for 'Cashier':*

Accept Silver.

In the window of a Japanese store:

We wish you are Merry Christmas.

*Philippines photographic firm
specializing in bridal photos:*

You tie the knot,
we freeze you.

Store in Tokyo:

Welcome to the best place
where makes you happy.

*Advertisement for a wedding shop
in the* Enfield Independent *(London, UK):*

Bridesmaids from £65.

*Sign in the window of a shop
in Hadleigh, Suffolk, UK:*

Any underage person found trying to purchase
cigarettes or alcohol is liable to be banded
from these premises.

---

*Price is a very important factor
in any purchase . . .*

*Hong Kong store,
advertising a final clearance:*

Anal Clearance.

*Cards handed out
in front of shop, Mexico:*

Come to Juan's Jewelry Shop.
We won't screw you too much.

*Shop in Sapporo,
Japan announcing a sale:*

Beat the price off!

In the window of an Indian shop:

Why go somewhere else to be cheated
when you can come here?

All Part of the Package

Never judge a book by its cover, they say.
But should you judge a product by its packaging?

On a Japanese food processor:
Not to be used for the other use.

On a Japanese toothpaste:
Gives you strong mouth and refreshing wind!

Warning label on a Chinese lint-cleaning roller:

1. Do not use this roller to the floorings
that made of wood and plastic.

2. Do not use this roller to clean the stuffs that
dangerous to your hands such as glass and chinaware.

3. Do not use the roller to people's head,
it is dangerous that hair could be sticked up
to cause unexpected suffering.

Various product names from around the world:

Clean Finger Nail – Chinese tissues

Kolic – Japanese mineral water

Creap Creamy Powder – Japanese Coffee Creamer

Last Climax – Japanese tissues

Ass Glue – Chinese glue

Swine – Chinese chocolates

Libido – Chinese soda

Ban Cock – Indian cockroach repellent

Shocking – Japanese chewing gum

Homo sausage – East Asian fish sausage

Cat Wetty – Japanese moistened hand towels

Hornyphon – Austrian video recorder

Chocolate Colon – Japanese cookie

Shitto – Ghanian pepper sauce

Pipi – Yugoslavian orangeade

Polio – Czechoslovakian laundry detergent

Superglans – Netherlands car wax

I'm Dripper – Japanese instant coffee

Zit – Greek soft drink

My Fanny – Japanese toilet paper

Colon Plus – Spanish detergent

On a range of products produced by a Japanese company:
Too fast to live, too young to happy.

Russian ammunition box:
Hurting cartridges.

Thai amplifier:
The whisper amplifier device is a micro one used
for someone who rare to hear or interception.

Clockwork toy made in Hong Kong:
Guaranteed to work throughout its useful life.

Japanese toy:
Danger! A dangerous toy. This toy is being
made for the extreme priority the good looks.
The little part which suffocates when the sharp part
which gets hurt is swallowed is contained generously.
Only the person who can take responsibility
by itself is to play.

*A game made in China called 'Top Bingo',
which lists its charms as:*

Free More Funny!

Increase Brain.

Interesting.

Amused.

---

*Food packaging is a particular bane of modern life.
Days can pass as you try in vain to get at your
Red Leicester. At least now you've got something
to laugh at during the struggle . . .*

Crème brûlée in a Paris supermarket:

Preheat your oven on grill, strew your cream
with sugar. Knock over the recipient to get rid
of the excess. Let the cream warm for few minutes
before eating.

Jar of jam in India:

Contains no fruit whatsoever.

Instructions on a packet of convenience food from Italy:

Besmear a backing pan, previously buttered with a good tomato sauce, and, after, dispose the cannelloni, lightly distanced between them in a only couch.

Japanese low-fat yoghurt:

For Gourmet and Ladies.

On a Japanese Coca-Cola can:

I feel Coke & sound special.

On a Japanese chocolate bar:

Soft and mild, like a Japanese woman. Good flavor and full of juice.

On a Japanese tea bag:

Do not wet with water.

On a Russian ice-cream bar:

Do not taste our Ice Cream when it is too hard.
Please continue your conversation until the
Ice Cream grows into a softer. By adhering
this advisement you will fully appreciate
the wonderful Soviet Ice Cream.

On a Japanese food package:

This cute mild curry uses 100% Japanese apple
and cheerful hamster.

Label on the Japanese soft drink Pocari Sweat:

Highly recommended as a beverage
for such activities as sports, physical labor,
after a hot bath, and even as a eye-opener
in the morning.

UCC Mocha Blend Coffee label, Japan:

This coffee has the smooth
and harmonious taste
with full of aroma.

UCC Drink it Black Coffee label, Japan:

Black coffee has great features
which other coffees have never had:
Non-sugar.

*On a bag of sweets bought in Wardour Street,
London, UK:*

Sweet candy, taste of pure candy,
bring a pleasure.

*On a box of ChocoBouchees,
a Japanese chocolate dessert cake:*

Confidence of creating deliciousness.
This tastiness can not be carried
even by both hands.

Label on an orange-flavoured drink, Japan:

This light and smooth taste drink is the best
refreshment to you. Anytime, anywhere,
just like your friend.

Kasugai Fruit Gummy snacks, Japan:

The gorgeous taste of fully ripened pineapple,
imposing as a southern island king crowned
in glory, is yours to enjoy in every soft
and juice Kasugai Pineapple Gummy.
Its translucent color so alluring and taste
and aroma so gentle and mellow offer admiring
feelings of a graceful lady. Enjoy soft
and juicy Kasugai Muscat Gummy.

From a Tokyo trade guide:

Daily sweat is nullified by this admirable coffee
set at free chatting. You can afford to grind coffee
grains while having coffee itself & enjoying hand
works to powder, befitted to lay on the interior
item made of wooden at anywhere wanted to.
Coffee fragrance matches to the article
in a cute and quiet circumstance.

In an Italian advertising campaign:

Schweppes Toilet Water.

French cheese:

This crud is from the finest milk solely
from the cows of the Brie region.

Sign Language

There's something particularly beautiful about a sign that's got lost in translation. All that effort, all that metal, all that paint – but no one stopped to check the words . . .

Sign on the grass in a Paris park:

Please do not be a dog.

Temple in Burma:

Footwearing strictly prohibited.

Indian national park:

NOTICE:
Ramganga River is inhabited by crocodiles.
Swimming is prohibited.
Survivors will be prosecuted.

Tibet:

Reception Centre for the Unorganised Tourists.

Street sign in Japan:

Waiting Will Be Prosecuted.

Sign in Le Touquet, France:

Instructions to Users of the ascenseur,
Persons ignorant of the maneuvers of the ascenseur
are prayed instantly to address themselves
to the concierge.

Sign posted in Germany's Black Forest:

It is strictly forbidden on our Black Forest camping site that people of different sex, for instance, men and women, live together in one tent unless they are married with each other for that purpose.

On a tap in a Finnish washroom:

To stop the drip, turn cock to right.

At the Eiffel Tower:

Renovating with curtsy to history: The elevator in the East pier is currently being widely upgraded. The current renovation involves updating these controls to the latest state of the art. Société Nouvelle d'exploitation de la Tour Eiffel apologises for all the temporary inconveniences.

Chinese sign:

Little grass is smiling slightly, please walk on the pavement.

Amusement ride, Saudi Arabia:

For your safety this game is not allowed
for those who suffer from hearts, diabetics,
nerves, high pressure and pregnants.

Bank in Bucharest, Romania:

Count change over the counter.
Ulterior complaints are not listened.

*The government in Seoul, South Korea,
established a hotline for taxi passengers
who encountered rudeness.
A sign in taxis advised of this:*

Intercourse Discomfort Report Center.

In a temple in Bangkok, Thailand:

It is forbidden to enter a woman
even a foreigner if dressed as a man.

A private school in Nairobi, Kenya:
No trespassing without permission.

Oklahoma City, USA:
No dumping – trespassers will be violated.

Calcutta (Kolkata), India:
Do not spit here and there.

And another:
Commit no nuisance.

Japanese 'Do not enter' sign:
Don't get into this.

Malaysia:
Caution water on road during rain.

Tai Wo station, Hong Kong:

The toilets will be partially suspended for use.

Spanish rental apartment:

Deposit: The owner asks for a deposit
of 25.000 ptas as a guarantee for the flat.
This amount will be returned at the end
of your stay if any damage has been done.

Ski chalet, Nagano, Japan:

Let's skiing.

Bus station, Laos:

Figure out fare office.

Museum of the Revolution, Havana, Cuba:

The museum are making different constructions work.
Please we entreat excuse.

Saldanha Bay, South Africa:

Warning!
To all seagulls swimming in red water
is strictly prohibited.

*Log Flume ride, Europa Park amusement park,
near Freiburg, Germany:*

Do not leaning or reaching out of the boat
is stridly forbidden.

Museum in Shanghai, China:
Be careful to butt head on wall.

Liaocheng, China:
Care the stairs.

Next to a bin in Wuhan, China:
Poisonous and evil rubbish.

Plastic sign warning Japanese passers-by
of ongoing work on electric cabling:
Execution in progress.

In a small town outside Beijing, China:
Welcome to tourism holiday spot Hurauo
and expect everything to turn out as you wish.

Outside a Japanese office block:

The most finest address.

*Resort at Iguaco Falls on the border
between Argentina and Paraguay:*

We offer you peace and seclusion.
The paths to our resort are only passable by asses.
Therefore, you will certainly feel at home here.

At Mallorca airport:

Distinguished Visitor: It is known that all the turistic
services in Mallorca are maintaining a correct relation
price quality, but even though, we wish to prize
the establishments and services that to the opinion
of our visitors, surpass notoriously for their quality.

To be able to fill out these questionnaires you must
write the name of this establishment, installation
or turistic service, as is shown below, and you must
give a punctuation between 6 and 10 points hoping
that the service that you must punctuate has been
the best in the relation price-quality.

Florence, Italy:

You are in a monumental palace,
alike an Ufitzi's galley of Florence.
You are therefore kindly requested
to behave consequently.

Tourist site in Beijing:

No fight, scrap, scrabble, rabble, feudal,
fetish or sexy service.

Yudu scenic spot in China:

Please don't surpass the cautionary driftwood
while having the aquatic visiting.

Kyoto Imperial Palace, Japan:

If a tour group contains more than the number
stiputed above, it is different in application.
The particulars will be asked the clerk at the window.
A man below 18 years old should be accompanied
by the adults.

Rules for climbing Mount Fuji, Japan:

A teffific gust often overtakes three times consecutively. Keep yourself lying flat on the siope until it's completely blown over.

Danger comes soonest when it's despised.

In case of bad weather such as, storm, fain, snow and a dense fog, avoid climbing futher than the fifth staition. when the weather breaks suddely. just give up half-way and return.

The nearest-to-the-sky location in Japan is far colder than the feets of the mountain.

Bring garbage back to your home.

Cash machine in China:

Help oneself terminating machine.

Chinese temple:

Please take one step forward and crap twice.

*Some locations seem to possess a special genius
for befuddled signs. Swimming pools,
for instance . . .*

Hotel pool, Istanbul, Turkey:

No diving. No nakedness. No ruining.

France:

Swimming is forbidden
in the absence of the savior.

Eldorado, Santa Fe, New Mexico:

Violations will be enforced.

Plantation Bay resort, Philippines:

Swimming pool suggestions:
Open 24 hours.
Lifeguard on duty 8 a.m. to 8 p.m.
Drowning absolutely prohibited.

Sri Lanka:

Do not use the diving board
when the swimming pool is empty.

Lifts have a similar talent . . .

Leipzig, Germany:

Do not enter the lift backwards,
and only when lit up.

Hotel in Tokyo, Japan:

Do not open door until door opens first.

Hotel in Belgrade, Serbia:

To move the cabin, push button for wishing floor.
If the cabin should enter more persons, each one
should press a number of wishing floor.
Driving is then going alphabetically
by national order.

Serbia:

Let us know about an unficiency
as well as leaking on the service.
Our utmost will improve it.

Tokyo:

Keep your hands away
from unnecessary
buttons for you.

Also zoos . . .

Phuket, Thailand:

Common Wild Pig
Don't Eat The Animals

Budapest, Hungary:

Please do not feed the animals.
If you have any suitable food,
give it to the guard on duty.

Japan:

Children found straying
will be taken to the lion house.

Czech Republic:

No smoothen the lion.

. . . and finally, the Great Wall of China:

The most magnificent strange stone city in China
Don't climb on the U-shaped opens.

At a zip-wire slide near the Great Wall, Simatai:

1. Those who suffer from high blood pressure,
   mental disease, horrifying of highness
   and liquour heads are refused.

2. Those who are above 65 years old
   and the disabled are refused.

3. Each set of belt for one person only.
   Hold tightly the belt when you are seated.

4. When you are using the belt,
   please follow the instruction of the staff.
   Never use only by yourself.

5. Take good care of your personal belongings
   to avoid the drop-off from your hand.

Romantic Ramblings

———

*That old devil called love has had us all in its spell
at one time or another. Finding the right words
to describe how we feel can be a challenge.
For some people, it's a real challenge . . .*

Israeli lonely-hearts advertisement:

41, with 18 years of teaching in my behind.
Looking for American-born woman
who speaks English very good.

*Message on an Internet dating site,
from a Thai woman to her prospective partner:*

I started go aerobic dance, because I am fat.
I think, when you come Thailand,
you want to see me on slim body!

Russian woman's lonely-hearts advertisement:

I am looking for an realy educated man
who can be joke to himself.

———

*Sometimes, whole relationships
can get lost in translation . . .*

*Text message from an Italian boyfriend
to his English girlfriend:*

Here is coldest. I need your familiar
worm burning kisses.

And another:

Are you like spend your free time in contry
or in town? shopping or walking on the hilly,
or long the cost on the beach. or just seat look
the landscape. I did like know more about you,
that i try to make for you my best. let my know
about you We had so little time (so nice),
i would like spend more e more time with you
I remember your eyes,(bellissimi)
last things i was looked in you.
Beautyfull memory.

He's still going:

Life is very peaky for me here but knowing that someone is on the other side of the sleeve sea is thinking on me makes me strong.

Now he's been to the doctor and is suffering from . . .

high blond pressure.

Things are tense between the Italian and his girlfriend.
He suggests a tête-à-tête to resolve matters.
Or rather, he suggests an . . .

air-cleaning vis a vis.

Miscellaneous Musings

---

*Some of the things that get lost in translation defy
not just understanding, they defy categorization . . .*

*Taiwanese poster publicizing
Guinness World of Records exhibition:*

In this kaleidoscopic world, nothing is too strange,
extraordinary men and affairs, including all
phenomena. Welcome to 'surprising world of
Guinness World of Records Museum to enjoy
the records' maintainers' live performances
and world folk-custom show.

*American advertisement
for Scandinavian vacuum cleaner:*

Nothing sucks like an Electrolux.

*The American slogan for Salem cigarettes is 'Salem –
Feeling Free'. In Japan, this was translated as:*

When smoking Salem, you will feel so refreshed
that your mind seems to be free and empty.

*Translation of 'Permanent Under-Secretary'
on Japanese business card:*

Everlasting typist.

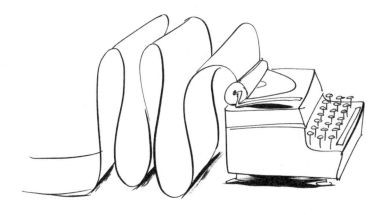

Portuguese patent agent:

It will not be necessary to state the name
and address of the inventor if the applicant
is not himself.

In 1855 Pedro Carolino published The New Guide
of the Conversation *in Portuguese and English.
Unfortunately, Carolino didn't actually speak any English –
he wrote the book by referring to a Portuguese-French phrase
book, then a French-English dictionary.
The 'conversation' section included:*

Apply you at the study
during that you are young.

I am catched cold in the brain.

If can't please at everyone one's.

I dead myself in envy to see her.

This girl have a beauty edge.

Do no might one's understand to speak.

The vocabulary section included:

OF THE MAN:

The brain

The brains

The fat of the leg

The ham

The inferior lip

The superior lip

The entrails

The reins

DEFECTS OF THE BODY:

A blind

A lame

A bald

A left handed

An ugly

A squint-eyed

A scurf

A deaf

President Heinrich Lubke,
welcoming Queen Elizabeth II
to West Germany in the 1960s:

Who are you?

On the same trip, at the theatre (attempting to tell her
that the performance would begin any minute):

Equal goes it loose.

Sewage treatment plant,
as marked on a Tokyo map:

Dirty Water Punishment Place.

Advertisement in US Asia Times
for a professional interpreter:

Are you unable to express your in English?
I can help you in the right earnest.

Translation agency's advertisement
in the Moscow Times*:*

Bet us your letter of business translation do.
Every people in our staffing know English like the
hand of their back. Up to the minuet wise-street
phrases, don't you know, old boy.

Liverpool FC slogan 'You'll Never Walk Alone',
as printed on a shirt in Liaocheng, China:

You'll Never Pickle Again.

Madras (Chennai, India) newspaper:

Our editors are colleged and write like
the Kipling and the Dickens.

*Norwegian Prime Minister
after a service in Brazil:*

Thank you for the mess.

Newly appointed Danish minister:

I am in the beginning of my period.

German-English textbook:

After a certain time cheques are stale
and cannot be cashed.

Helpful words and phrases
listed in Learn Greek with Me,
an English-Greek dictionary:

Bring me a partion of . . .

Only half a partion of . . .

Smocking/No Smocking.

Bring me, we are in a harry!

Greek flavourable sweets and candies.

Chocolates: plain, milk, Pavlidoo, bitter.

This is to go at deffered rate (halt rate).

I cannot speek.

In a Paris guidebook:

To call a broad from France,
first dial 00.

Japanese-English conversation textbook:

mother – brother – sister – ground father –
ground mother . . .

Italian reader's review
of About A Boy *by Nick Hornby:*

It is the perfect kind of reading for having some relax and enjoying one's own free time. Despite the subject of it might seem trivial, it provides indeed some interesting starting points for reflecting on some issues of our life, which often seem more troublesome of what they deserve to be.

Italian furniture advertisement:

Big leather pieces only joint by an intangible stitching create a perfect balance of proportions.

Cairo, Egypt, Internet café:

Please you are not allowed to enter or open the following sites: a, the sexual sites; b, religion sites; c, political sites. Thank you for your co-operator.

Russian chess book:

A lot of water has been passed under the bridge since this variation has been played.

Advertisement in an Indian newspaper:

For sale to kind master: Full grown tigress, goes daily walk untied, and eats flesh from hand.

From the Soviet Weekly:

There will be a Moscow Exhibition of Arts by 15,000 Soviet Republic painters and sculptors. These were executed over the past two years.

Names of buildings in Bangkok, Thailand:

TIT Tower and PMT Mansion.

Business card pushed through a letter box
in Pattaya, Thailand:

Exceuse me!
Are You Toilet Full?
If it full. We take out for you.
If not it. O.K.

Financial institution in Detroit, USA:

Ask about our plans for owning your home.

On a Danish website for pesticides:

PESTS: Trips constitutes only a small problem.
Use utility animals or insecticide soap.
Eventually showering with water.

WATERING: Scarcely watering is recomended.
Tolerates drying out periodes between watering.
No special demand to the housewive's green thumbs.

Taxi driver in Cairo,
trying to chat up English tourists:

Jubbly lovely.

From a Japanese newspaper article:

Four people were killed, one seriously.

International dormitory in Kansai, Japan:

Do not bring the newspapers to your room.
It might disturb other residents.

An invitation to a picnic:

Join! You will meet strange people!

Advertisement in Beijing, China:

Our watches are waterproof,
shock-proof and time-proof.

*Notice to tenants of an apartment building
in Montreal, Canada:*

A thorough extermination of the building
is presently necessary.

From the Montreal Gazette:

Ordinary People has been falling in popularity
ever since Mary Tyler Moore's real life son
committed death.

At a Montreal club:

During the renovation of the main entrance,
members should use the old ladies' entrance.

*Card of 'recommandation' for a miniature golf course
in Ostend, the Netherlands:*

Level with the feet holes or mound
do by playing on the game.

No working players are invited to stay
on the stony mat.

On a T-shirt, Hong Kong:

Child be a public servant. The best balance
of music and technology within a vaguely.

On a Japanese T-shirt:

Polygon Form: It is a solid image by the line
and plane. Anyone is assembled on the screen.

On a French pest-control firm's website:

Small animals nibble you the life?
They give you the cockroach?

Brochure for Odaiba, Japan:

Some people just think that Odaiba is just like
a double sided magic mirror. Yes, exactly.
Whatever dream you have, you may find its trace
and realize it in Odaiba. Just tour through Odaiba
by Free Shuttle Bus. To your surprise,
you may make new friends.

East African newspaper:

A new swimming pool is rapidly taking shape
since the contractors have thrown in the bulk
of their workers.

*Sign in the Netherlands advertising
a Dutch-English grammar tutor:*

Englisch as she is goodly pocken.

Label on an electric shower, Thailand:

Shower of happiness.
Total safety guaranteed.

Marketing mailshot from a Spanish company:

Half statement of press publishes and distributes
free sectors publications of the most representative
Spanish industry in order to collaborating exporter
of the products and manufactured of happiness
in the expansion companies, for the one which
we have considered you could be of their interest
know to the detail the reference of the fabric
industrial Spaniard, of the that they are facilitated
the reasons social, complete adresses and description
of the productive activity for medium from
journalistic reports.

Brochure for an amusement park in Odaiba:

In this real environment replicated entertainment park,
you can enjoy the very things of Hongkong
by just stepping your foot one step in. Here lies
the amazing experience never elsewhere.

Taiwanese advertisement for a laptop computer:

Take it to take off away from where other majority
has stayed long since. Not only abreast it keeps you
but also ahead of the cornfield of computing.

Brochure for Odayku Museum, Japan:

There are a newspaper publishing company
and a special exibition by own company plan.
Be planned a wide genre from a picture
to a photograph by richness.

Brochure for Idemitsu Museum, Japan:

Have formality of the first kabuki play ground.
There is the earphone guide who can hear explanation
which enjoying the play.

Italian marketing mailshot:

This publication has dedicated the necklace of nature
classical hybrid and is extensive in four tongues to
scholastic custom, whose production, that to full
rhythm will be of menstrual lilt, satisfies the Italian
market, for which we retain, might fully interest
you it am because the commodity is economic.

Libyan leader Colonel Muammar Gaddafi:

I never use shampoo with milk or eggs.
These are imperialist ideas.

From a Japanese website:

The contents of this website make service
offer in Japan now.

The direction which does not understand Japanese
well is this advanced ON prohibition.

*Message from a successful eBay bidder (in Japan)
to the item's seller (in America):*

I was not seeing your explanation well.
Very much I was excused as for the remittance
to you, I remitted Pursuit is produced easily
by the cord in the time that EMS forwarded
even from America. The number is early
to be linked to the arrival to you and be late
on 5th I am scheduled to arrive within 9 days.
Please send the destination to my parents' home.
Please the my best regards.

*Note left for an English visitor who had taken
his Dutch hosts their favourite products,
including loose tobacco:*

Dear Pete,
Thank you for the chocolate,
the coffee and the shag.

*Business letter sent out when Götabanken
changed its name to Gota Bank:*

Dear friends,
we are the same guys as before,
although we have lost our pricks.

Japanese graffiti:
FACK YOU MAN

Advertisement in Angling Times
(UK magazine):

Executioner Pole, 13m, unused,
used twice.

*Covering letter with application
submitted to London employment agency:*

I am an Italian boy, me they are as soon as graduated
in Banking Economy at University of Siena and it
would appeal to a lot to make experience to me in
England. They are one dynamics person, of sociable
open nature and; I pursue mine objects to you with

decision, they attract the challenges very to me and I face every experience with the maximum engagement. I wish to improve itself continuously is from the human point of view that professional increasing in such a way my baggage of acquaintance and experience. I have numerous interests between which sport and music.

More CV mishaps:

My intensity and focus are at inordinately high levels and my ability to complete projects on time is unspeakable.

Education: Curses in liberal arts, curses in computer science, curses in accounting.

Instrumental in ruining entire operation for a Midwest chain store.

I am a rabid typist.

Proven ability to track down and correct erors.

Strengths:
Ability to meet deadlines while maintaining composer.

I demand a salary commiserate with my extensive experience.

I have lurnt Word Perfect 6.0,
computor and spreadsheat progroms.

Received a plague for Salesperson of the Year.

Reason for leaving last job: maturity leave.

Personal interests:
Donating blood. Fourteen gallons so far.

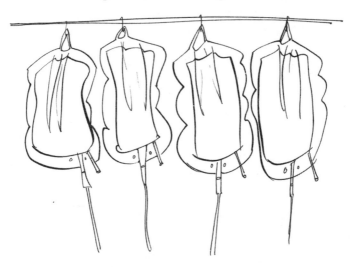

Wholly responsible for two (2) failed financial
institutions.

Failed bar exam with relatively high grades.

Let's meet, so you can ooh and aah
over my experience.

You will want me to be Head Honcho in no time.

I Am a perfectionist and rarely if if ever
forget details.

I am loyal to my employer at all costs.

Reason for leaving last job: They insisted that all
employees get to work by 8:45 every morning.
Could not work under those conditions.

The company made me a scapegoat,
just like my three previous employers.

Finished eighth in my class of ten.

And from a covering letter:

Thank you for your consideration.
Hope to hear from you shorty!

*Slogan on mugs produced by Warwickshire County Cricket
Club, who wanted to bill their star bowler 'King of Spin':*

Ashley Giles – King of Spain.

From an eBay advertisement for a Chinese stamp album:

Contains stamps on more than 30 different subjects,
which are listed chronically in 20+ well printed
thick pages.

Fraudulent e-mail, purporting to be from Barclays Bank:

Technical services of the Barclays are upgrading
the software. Our new security system will help you
to avoid frequently transactions and to keep your
investments in safety. Due to technical update
we ask you to confirm your online banking
membership details.

Spam e-mail:

Your girl is unsatisfied with your pottency?
Don't wait until she finds another men!
Click here to choose from a great variety
of licensed love tabs! Best prises,
fast shipping and guaranteed effect!
Here you buy it right from warehouse!

And finally . . .

*Name of the author of this book,
as listed on a Japanese website
in the run-up to publication:*

Charlie Crocker.